WARBIRDS ILLUSTRATED NO. 29

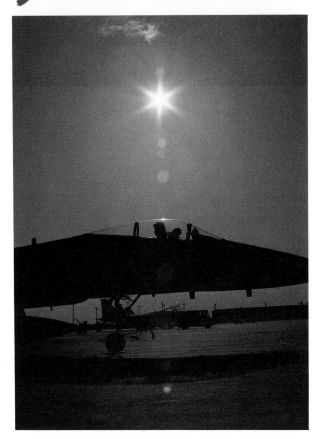

WARBIRDS ILLUSTRATED NO. 29

USAF
Today

DANA BELL

ARMS AND ARMOUR PRESS
London—Melbourne—Harrisburg, Pa.—Cape Town

Introduction

Warbirds Illustrated 29: USAF Today
Published in 1984 by Arms and Armour Press, Lionel
Leventhal Limited, 2–6 Hampstead High Street,
London NW3 1QQ; 11 Munro Street, Port
Melbourne 3207, Australia; Sanso Centre, 8 Adderley
Street, P.O. Box 94, Cape Town 8000, South Africa;
Cameron and Kelker Streets, P.O. Box 1831,
Harrisburg, Pennsylvania 17108, USA

British Library Cataloguing in Publication Data:
Bell, Dana
USAF today. – (Warbirds illustrated; no. 29)
1. United States. *Air Force* – History
2. Airplanes, Military – United States – History
I. Title   II. Series
623.74'6'0973   UG1243
ISBN 0-85368-679-3

Editing and layout by Roger Chesneau.
Printed and bound in Great Britain by
William Clowes Limited, Beccles and London.

One difficulty with any book that attempts to be current is that things are bound to change before it can be brought into print. So it is that *USAF Today* has already become a history – a history of the year 1983 to be exact. We can hope that this will prove to be the first of many such recent histories in the *Warbirds Illustrated* series.

Structuring a book around photographs always has the drawback that many important events are not well documented by the camera, but other, lesser events may be supported by hundreds of beautiful images. The weight of photos in this book does not therefore suggest, for example, that Exercise 'Team Spirit' is more important than 'Autumn Forge'; 'Team Spirit' simply offered a better graphic selection. Generally, photographs which tend to reflect the overall story of the USAF, regardless of where or when they were taken, have been selected. Photographers' names, when known, are individually credited. I have always felt that USAF photographers deserve credit for their work as much as talented camera-carrying civilians do. Again, the number of any particular individual's photos included in this book should be interpreted as a judgement only about which photos best tell the story, and not about individual ability.

This book would not have been possible without the help of three members of my old unit, the 1361st Audiovisual Squadron: Dave Tripp, Jonathan Arms and S/Sgt Pablo Marmelejo, who opened their files to me. Lt. Col. Eric Solander and Lt. Peter Meltzer of the Air Force Magazine and Book Branch offered their support to help me fill the pages, and independent photographers Don Linn and Al Lloyd supplied a number of important photographs from their libraries. Last but not least, a special 'thank you' goes to Susan, my red rover, for her love and support.

Dana Bell

◄3
Cover illustration: A single 'ship' from the USAF's 'Thunderbirds' display team climbs to altitude. (USAF)
1. (Half-title page) In 1982, the 48th FIS became the first air defence unit to convert to F-15s. Pilots can rotate to regular tactical units, but fly daily operational missions maintaining US air sovereignty. (Author)
2. (Title spread) An F-15A chase plane tops up its tanks during a B-1 test mission. (T/Sgt. William B. Belcher, USAF)
3. Sunset paints the contrails of an MAC C-141B. (USAF)

▲4

▲5

4. 'Brim Frost' is an annual military exercise held in Alaska which in January 1983 involved over 16,000 active duty, Reserve, and National Guard personnel in intensive, cold-weather combat training. Here, a fuel tank is mounted on the wing of a 388th Tactical Fighter Wing (TFW) F-16 at Eielson Air Force Base. (T/Sgt. W. Boyd Belcher, USAF)

5. A 62nd Military Airlift Wing (MAW) C-130 from McChord AFB, Washington, performs a Low Altitude Parachute Extraction System (LAPES) cargo drop at Clear Creek, Alaska. (Sgt. Kuck, USAF)

6. Strategic Air Command (SAC) KC-10 Extenders augment Air Force airlift capabilities in addition to their normal aerial refuelling duties. (Sgt. Kuck, USAF)

7. A-10s bank in the Alaskan sunset. (Sgt. Kuck, USAF)

6▲ 7▼

▲8 ▼9

8. One of the F-111Ds of the 522nd TFS, 27th TFW, which deployed from Cannon AFB, New Mexico for 'Brim Frost '83'. (AIC Emmett L. Stinson, USAF)

9. When the 43rd TFS of the 21st TFW converted from F-4Es to F-15s in 1982, unit tailcodes changed from 'FC' to 'AK'. (S/Sgt. Lou Hernandez, USAF)

10. 'Ostfriesland II', the second exercise named after the German dreadnought sunk by Billy Mitchell's bombers in the 1920s, placed F-15s, RF-4s, and E-3s on naval reconnaissance patrols off the coast of Okinawa. The training, which occupied two days in early February 1983, was enhanced by the presence of Soviet warships, which were on patrols of their own. In this photograph, two F-15s overfly a Soviet 'Kanin' class destroyer, with the carrier *Minsk* and a second destroyer barely visible in the background mists. (S/Sgt. Glenn B. Lindsey, USAF)

11. Two 18th TFW aircraft pass *Minsk*. (S/Sgt. Carl S. McGill, USAF)

12. Sortie completed, five of the American aircraft head for home. (S/Sgt. Carl S. McGill, USAF)

10▲

11▲ 12▼

▲13

13. A single F-15 banks over a stormy green sea. The 18th TFW began painting the Samurai warriors between the tails of its Japan-based Eagles in 1982. (S/Sgt. Glenn B. Lindsey, USAF)

14. 'Team Spirit' is an annual training operation involving US and Korean forces – it is the Free World's largest combat training exercise. Each March USAF units deploy from home bases to Pacific Air Forces (PACAF) units stationed in South Korea and Japan. The Civil Reserve Air Fleet (CRAF) is a partnership between twenty-one US commercial air carriers and the Military Airlift Command. In time of war or national emergency, more than 300 passenger and cargo aircraft can double MAC's strategic airlift capacity. This World Airways DC-10 is being loaded with cargo for the 563rd TFS's deployment from George AFB, California, to Korea. (T/Sgt. Rob Marshall, USAF)

▼14

15. An Army truck is unloaded from a Flying Tigers Airlines Boeing 747-100F somewhere in Korea. (T/Sgt. Dave Craft, USAF)
16. Sixteen F-15s of the 18th TFW's 67th TFS deploy from Kadena AFB, Okinawa, to Kwang Ju, Korea, at the beginning of 'Team Spirit '83'. (S/Sgt. Lono Kollars, USAF)

17. F-16s of the 35th TFS, 8th TFW ('The Wolf Pack'), refuel from a KC-135A. (S/Sgt. Glenn Lindsey, USAF)
18. A trio of 80th TFS F-16s over South Korea. (T/Sgt. Bert Mau, USAF)
19. An F-16 of the 35th TFS en route to a bombing run. A practice Sidewinder is mounted on the port wing rail, and three 500lb practice bombs hang beneath each wing. (S/Sgt. Glenn Lindsey, USAF)
20. SAC weapons technicians load mines into the bomb bay of a B-52D at Andersen AFB, Guam. (SRA Erik Baker, USAF)
21. Mines tumble from a B-52D during training off the South Korean coast. The last -D models of the B-52 were stricken from the Air Force inventory in late 1983. (M/Sgt. Mike Daniels, USAF)

▲17

▲18 ▼19

▲22

22. Wild Weasels from the 363rd TFS prepare for take-off from George AFB, California, for 'Team Spirit '83'. (T/Sgt. Rob Marshall, USAF)
23. Aircrews board an F-4C of the Hawaii Air National Guard (154th Composite Group) during missions from hardened Korean shelters. (T/Sgt. Bert Mau, USAF)
24. An RF-4C of the 18th TFW banks during a reconnaissance flight. Months later, the 18th became an all-F-15 unit. (M/Sgt. Mike Daniels, USAF)
25. Another unit deploying for 'Team Spirit' was the 356th TFS, 354th TFW, from Myrtle Beach AFB, South Carolina. (T/Sgt. Dave Craft, USAF)

▼23

▲26   27▶

26. 8th TFW armourers fuse 500lb bombs beneath the wing of one of the unit's F-16s. (T/Sgt. Bert Mau, USAF)

27. PJ and subject ride a jungle penetrator to a hovering HH-3 while a CH-3 circles. Note the chaff dispenser on the aft fuselage of the HH-3. (Sgt. Kuck, USAF)

28. An Air Force CH-3 sports new 'European One' camouflage paint above the Korean countryside. (T/Sgt. Dave Craft, USAF)

29. Korean and USAF combat controllers at the Sampoo drop zone, with Army UH-1s crossing in the background. (T/Sgt. Dave Craft, USAF)

30. An A-10 makes a gun run on mock targets at the Punsan range as part of a demonstration for US and Korean officials. (S/Sgt. Lono Kollars, USAF)

31. An air drop pallet is extracted by parachute from a C-130E. (T/Sgt. Dave Craft, USAF)

▼28

29▲

30▲ 31▼

32. (Previous spread) The first 'Copper Flag' exercises were held at Tyndall AFB, Florida, in March 1983, beginning a series of air defence exercises similar to the 'Red Flag' tactical training missions held in Nevada. Participants included the 5th FIS (F-106s from Minot AFB, North Dakota), the 48th FIS (F-15s from Langley AFB, Virginia), the 178th FIS (F-4Cs from the 119th FIG, North Dakota ANG) and the 194th FIS (F-106s from the 144th FIW, California ANG). This is a view of the Tyndall flight line during 'Copper Flag'. (USAF)

33. A weapons control system specialist of the 5th FIS checks a technical order in the cockpit of one of his squadron's F-106s. (USAF)

34. A 5th FIS F-106 takes off from Tyndall. In the background are PQM-102s, former front-line interceptors now used as target drones. (USAF)

35. A 5th FIS F-106 prepares for a night mission. (USAF)

36. The USAF began 1983 with approximately 64,000 women out of a total military force of almost 580,000. Although US law prohibits women from being assigned to combat jobs, they serve in nearly every non-combat position. This 48th FIS crew chief is running a post-flight check on her F-15. (USAF)

▲37

37. A tech sergeant of the 119th FIG checks the tail of his F-4C prior to take-off. 'The Happy Hooligans' nickname has been used by the group since the early 1960s. (USAF)

38. 119th FIG F-4Cs rest under protective covers on the Tyndall hardstand. (USAF)

39. The 'Thunderbirds' aerial demonstration team converted to

F-16s in 1983, a scheduled change which was not related to the 1982 crash of four team members in a T-38 training flight. The aircraft are combat-ready and need only a coat of paint before action – squadron members would if required fight with the 430th TFS of Nellis AFB's 474th TFW. Here, a four-ship diamond climbs against the blue desert sky. (S/Sgt. Bill Thompson, USAF)

▼38   39▶

▲40 ▼41

40. Diving inverted towards the desert floor, the 'Thunderbirds' mark their course with smoke. (S/Sgt. Bill Thompson, USAF)

41. A six-ship wedge approaches the top of a loop against the backdrop of a Nevada sunset. (S/Sgt. Bill Thompson, USAF)

42. All six of the 'Thunderbirds' F-16As over the desert not far from Nellis AFB, Nevada. The Commander of TAC, a former team member and leader of the 'Thunderbirds', took personal interest in perfecting the design of the team's red, white and blue colour scheme. (S/Sgt. Bill Thompson, USAF)

43. 'Thunderbirds' maintenance crews prepare aircraft No. 2 for another demonstration. Full combat equipment remains aboard the aircraft and is kept in working order to support the team's combat readiness obligations. (USAF)

44. Five members of the 'Thunderbirds' turn on the hardstand prior to a training mission. (USAF)

45. Diamond formation. (USAF)

46. Diamond formation flypast with landing gear extended. (USAF)

▲47

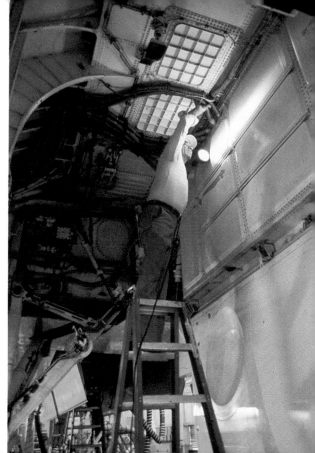

▲48 ▼49

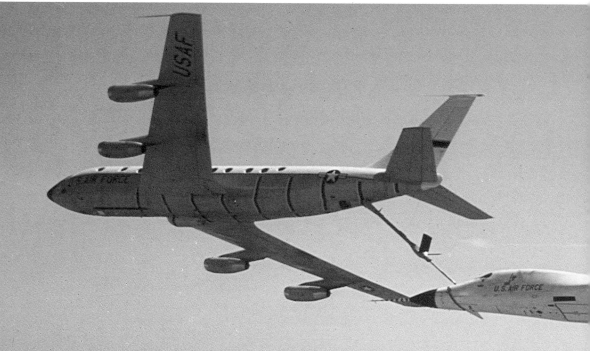

47. Resurrection of the B-1 strategic bomber programme will lead to the production of 100 B-1Bs by mid-1988, and in order to develop new systems two B-1As were brought out of mothballs early in 1983. B-1A No. 2's tail markings reflect its role in the B-1B test programme at Edwards AFB, Calfornia. (T/Sgt. William B. Belcher, USAF)

48. A civilian technician checks the main landing gear well of a B-1A prior to a test flight. (T/Sgt. William B. Belcher, USAF)

49. High above the Californian desert, a B-1A refuels from an Aeronautical Systems Division (ASD, of Air Force Systems Command) NKC-135. Note the camera pod at the root of the 135's right wing. (T/Sgt. William B. Belcher, USAF)

50. Also under test at Edwards was the Advanced Fighter Technology Integration (AFTI) F-16, sporting new canards and internal electronics. (USAF)

▲51

▲52 ▼53

51. The AFTI F-16 flanked by a pair of Edwards F-16As. The year 1983 saw the beginning and end of 'ED' tailcodes for chase planes of the Flight Test Center. (Reynolds, USAF)

52. Also new in the USAF inventory in 1983 was the UH-60A. Nine airframes from Army Blackhawk production were re-painted in USAF colours for aircrew training and familiarization. The HH-60D version on order for the Air Force will carry sophisticated night rescue equipment, miniguns and Stinger missiles, and an inflight refuelling probe. (USAF)

53. Rebuilding and re-engining KC-135As with General Electric/SNECMA CFM56 turbofans resulted in a new version of the Air Force's standard tanker – the KC-135R. The first of these aircraft began Operational Test and Evaluation (OT&E) at McConnell AFB, Kansas, in April 1983. The nose instrument boom will not be carried on operational tankers. The 'R' designation has been used previously, for a pair of KC-135s which flew special missions for SAC; the new KC-135Rs were originally known as KC-135REs, for 're-engined'. (USAF)

54. A similar re-engining programme mounts JT3D-3B engines on what are now known as KC-135Es. Intended for Air National Guard refuelling squadrons, this example is flown by the 150th ARS, New Jersey ANG. (Don Linn)

55. The newest staff transport in service is the C-20, a military version of the Grumman Gulfstream III. This airframe, assigned to the 89th MAW at Andrews AFB, District of Columbia, was one of the three leased during 1983 pending delivery of USAF contracts. (Miles R. Young, USAF)

56. Based on an AGM-69 SRAM booster rocket with special optical guidance systems, the ASAT (anti-satellite missile) began mock-up compatibility evaluations in 1983. Air Defense F-15s will carry the missiles to altitude for launch against space targets. (USAF)

54▲

55▲ 56▼

▲57

57. An EC-135, one of the US Air Forces Europe (USAFE) flying command posts, seen over RAF Mildenhall. Note the high visibility of the white-topped C-5A in the background. (T/Sgt. Jose Lopez, USAF)

58. The 81st TFW (tailcodes 'WR') flies six squadrons of A-10s from Britain and forward operating locations in Europe. This Warthog carries three Maverick training missiles. (T/Sgt. Jose Lopez, USAF)

▼58

59▲

60▲ **61**▼

59. A trio of F-5Es from the 527th Tactical Fighter Training Aggressor Squadron (TFTAS) based at RAF Alconbury. The squadron simulates Soviet aircraft and tactics to provide realistic combat training for NATO crews. (T/Sgt. Jose Lopez, USAF)

60. An F-111F of the 494th TFS, 48th TFW, banks to show four laser-guided 2,000lb bombs, a white ECM pod, and a new Pave Tack electro-optical target designator pod. (T/Sgt. Jose Lopez, USAF)

61. The 3rd Air Force's second F-111 wing is the 20th TFW, equipped with F-111Es. The blue tail tip marks the 55th TFS, whilst the blue bombs signify practice munitions. (T/Sgt. Jose Lopez, USAF)

62. Strategic Air Command bases TR-1s, U-2s and SR-71s with Det 4 of the 9th Strategic Reconnaissance Wing at RAF Mildenhall. Here an SR-71 moves out of that base through heavy fog. (T/Sgt. Jose Lopez, USAF)

63. An HH-53C of the 67th ARRSq flies over base housing at RAF Woodbridge. (T/Sgt. Jose Lopez, USAF)

64. The 57th Fighter Weapons Wing at Nellis AFB tested a twin Sidewinder mount on some of its A-10s in 1983. In 25 man-hours and at a hardware cost of under $2,000, the Warthog can gain an air-to-air capability guaranteed to give Soviet fighters something new to think about. (The Air Force has *not* announced plans to replace its F-15s with A-10s!) (USAF)

◄**62**

63▲ **64**▼

▲65

▲66 ▼67

65. An F-4E of the 526th TFS, 86th TFW, out of Ramstein AB, Germany. Air-to-air combat missiles include four Sidewinders and four Sparrows. (USAF)

66. The 52nd TAW out of Spangdahlem AB, Germany, flies a mixed force of F-4Ds, -Es, and -Gs. This is an E-model of the 23rd TFS; note the newly applied low-visibility star on the fuselage. (M/Sgt. Don Sutherland, USAF)

67. Another of the 52nd's Phantoms, an F-4G of the 81st TFS, banks over the River Mosel. Two Shrike anti-radiation missiles hang on wing pylons. (M/Sgt. Don Sutherland, USAF)

68. A new aircraft for the Air National Guard is the F-16, which was introduced to South Carolina's 169th TFG in 1983. (Don Linn)

69. A UH-1N of the 1st Helicopter Squadron over Maryland during 'Wounded Eagle' medical exercises. (Mickey Sanborn, USAF)

70. The same Huey as it appeared later in 1983, when the 1st began to adopt a new blue, gold and white colour scheme. (Miles R. Young, USAF)

68▲

69▲ 70▼

▲71 ▼72

71. SAC manages the E-4B National Emergency Airborne Command Post (NEACP, pronounced 'kneecap'!) which has been based at Andrews AFB, DC, since the mid-1970s. In 1983, SAC announced intentions to re-station these aircraft at an undisclosed base in the US Midwest. (USAF)

72. HH-53Hs were developed for MAC's combat rescue squadrons, but were transferred instead to TAC's 1st Special Operations Wing. The tables were turned in 1983 when all of TAC's Special Operations resources were transferred to MAC! Here an HH-53H refuels from an HC-130P of the 55th ARRSq. (T/Sgt. Ken Hammond, USAF)

73. A UH-1N of the 20th SOS banks over Hurlbert Field, Florida. The spotted paint scheme was applied in the late 1970s to simulate Soviet machines during helicopter-versus-helicopter combat experiments. (T/Sgt. Ken Hammond, USAF)

74. An MC-130E of MAC's 8th SOS (Special Operations Squadron) performs an aerial recovery with its Fulton system. Note the pick-up subject (extreme bottom right of photo) hanging from the end of the tether. (T/Sgt. Ken Hammond, USAF)

73 ▼

74 ▼

▲75 ▼76

75. MAC's entire C-141A fleet was modified to C-141B standard in a programme that ended in 1982. This March 1983 photograph shows the tail of a 437th MAW Starlifter tufted with strands of yarn to determine what effects the lengthened fuselage was having on airflow during airdrops. (T/Sgt. Ken Hammond, USAF)

76. An air-to-air view of the same aircraft shows the airflow to be laminar during a flight from Charleston AFB, South Carolina. (T/Sgt. Ken Hammond, USAF)

77. The 401st TFW, based at Torrejon AB, Spain, celebrated its 40th anniversary and the arrival of the unit's first F-16 on 5 April. Maintenance crews had been working on the Falcon since December 1982, but the April ceremony marked the first F-16 assigned to the unit. Here, questions are answered by a pilot during the public's introduction to the new arrival. (M/Sgt. Don Sutherland, USAF)

78. A 401st F-16, with the blue and white tail checks of the 612th TFS, goes through preflight prior to a mission. The starboard wingtip rail holds a training Sidewinder missile. (M/Sgt. Don Sutherland, USAF)

79. Pilot and crew chief in late afternoon shadows. The Fighting Falcon motif behind the cockpit is exclusive to the 401st TFW. (M/Sgt. Don Sutherland, USAF)

77 ▲

78 ▲ 79 ▼

▲80 ▼81

80. In April 1983 the 19th Tactical Air Support Squadron, based at Osan, Korea, began to replace its OV-10s with OA-37s. As the squadron commander completes his last OV-10 flight and accepts the unit's first OA-37, his pilots apply liberal doses of ceremonial baptismal fluids. (M/Sgt. Don Sutherland, USAF)

81. An Air Force staff sergeant prepares stencils during the repainting of one of the 19th's OA-37s. The base colour scheme is Gunship Gray. (T/Sgt. Bert Mau, USAF)

82. A repainted and re-marked OA-37 sits on the Osan ramp. (T/Sgt. Bert Mau, USAF)

83. A repainted and re-marked OA-37 makes a familiarization flight over Korea. (T/Sgt. Bert Mau, USAF)

84. The year 1983 saw the first application of 'European One' camouflage (green/green/grey) to the C-5A. Eventually, the entire fleet of 77 C-5As, as well as the 50 newly ordered C-5Bs, will display this 'flying pickle' colour scheme. This 60th MAW Galaxy was photographed over San Francisco. (S/Sgt. Bob Simons, USAF)

85. Big, green and ugly, a camouflaged C-5 darkens the sky over Lake Berryessa, California, July 1983. (S/Sgt. Bob Simons, USAF)

86. High over the Pacific, a C-5 refuels from an SAC KC-135. (M/Sgt. Richard M. Diaz. USAF)

87. US Defense Department policies have opened all non-combat jobs, including aircrew positions (particularly on strategic airlift aircraft such as the C-141), to women. In May, the first all-female flight crew to make an overseas flight delivered cargo from McGuire AFB, New Jersey, to Rhein-Main AB, Germany. The crew included (left to right) Capt. Guiliana Sangiorgio (aircraft commander), Capt. Barbara Akin (1st pilot), Lt. Terri Ollinger (co-pilot), Sgt. Mary Kath Eiche (loadmaster), T/Sgt. Donns Wertz (instructor flight engineer), S/Sgt. Denise Meunier (flight engineer), and AlC Bernadette Botti (loadmaster). (S/Sgt. Marvin D. Lynchard, USAF)

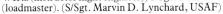

▲88

▲89 ▼90

88. Aircraft of the 62nd MAW, based at McChord AFB, Washington, fly over the torn crest of Mount St. Helens. C-130s and C-141s form the principle equipment of the 62nd. (Ken Hackman, USAF)

89. One of the 62nd's C-141Bs refuels from a 141st Aerial Refueling Wing KC-135A. (Ken Hackman, USAF)

90. A C-141B of the 437th MAW flies over Patriots Point near Charleston AFB, South Carolina. Ships below include *Yorktown* and the first nuclear-powered commercial vessel, the NS *Savannah*. (T/Sgt. Ken Hammond, USAF)

91. A C-141B of Charleston AFB's 437th MAW over South Carolina. (T/Sgt. Ken Hammond, USAF)

92. The Military Airlift Command's annual tactical airlift competition, 'Volant Rodeo', is held at Pope AFB, North Carolina. In June 1983, Air Guard, Reserve, and regular Air Force units were joined by Brazilian, Australian, Canadian, German, Italian, New Zealand and Portuguese teams. Here, a single Transall, the German entrant, sits among the multinational C-130s. (USAF)

▲93 ▼94

93. 82nd Airborne Division paratroopers depart from a C-130 during airdrop evaluations. The 82nd provided jumpers for all of the competition's paratroop drops. (USAF)

94. 'Balikatan Tangent Flash '83' was a Philippine/USAF military exercise testing the ability of the Filipinos to defend themselves from external threats. Part of that training included search and rescue missions. Here, PJs of the 31st ARRSq stand guard as 'injured' are moved to a waiting HH-3. (USAF)

95. D Flight of the 48th flies T-33 trainers as target aircraft for the F-15s. (Author)

96. Dusk patrol: take-off for a late-afternoon mission from the alert sheds. Ground crews make last-minute inspections before the Eagles launch. Alert aircraft carry live Sparrows, but no Sidewinders. (Author)

97. An F-15B of the 318th FIS moves to the reception area during ceremonies marking that unit's transition from F-106s. In June the 318th became the second Air Defense unit to fly the F-15. (Al Lloyd)

95▲

96▲ 97▼

98. In May 1983, SAC B-52Ds and Royal Australian Air Force
F-111Cs tested Australia's fighter defences during Exercise 'Pitch
Black'. Three B-52Ds of the 60th Bomb Squadron, joined by a trio of
Pacific Tanker Task Force KC-135s, deployed from Andersen AFB,
Guam, to Darwin RAAFB. The deployment was one of the last for
SAC's black-bellied D-models, the last of the ageing bombers being
retired in late 1983. This photograph shows bombers and tankers
on the Darwin flight line prior to an early-morning mission.
(USAF)
99. One of the 60th's B-52Ds closes on a tanker during refuelling
operations over the Pacific. (USAF)
100. Common refuelling equipment enabled the RAAF's F-111Cs to
top up from the same tankers as SAC's B-52s during Exercise 'Pitch
Black': probe and drogue systems would otherwise have
necessitated some tanker boom modifications prior to take-off.
(USAF)

▼98   99▶

▼100

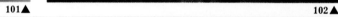

101. 'Global Shield' is the largest SAC annual training exercise. It is held at Ellsworth AFB, South Dakota, at the end of June. Here, B-52Hs of the 77th Bomb Squadron approach a tanker for refuelling. SAC's B-52Gs and -Hs will remain in service through to the 1990s until replaced by B-1Bs and other newer aircraft. (USAF)
102. Missile crews at Grand Forks AFB and Ellsworth AFB work on

Minuteman IIs in their silos. (S/Sgt. Louis Comeger, USAF)
103. During an early-morning, minimum-interval take-off (MITO), a KC-135 rises through the rains at Ellsworth. A highlight of 'Global Shield' was the fact that every non-alert aircraft launched without incident. (USAF)

▲104 ▼105

104. Exercise 'Checkered Flag' is TAC's training for overseas combat deployment. Unit leaders visit their assigned deployment bases yearly, entire squadrons making the trip once every three years. This is an aerial view of Ahlhorn AB, Germany, with hardened shelters, taken in mid-summer 1983. A-10s of Det 3, 81st TFW, were joined by A-10s of the 47th TFS (AFRES) which deployed from Barksdale AFB, Louisiana. (T/Sgt. Plummer, USAF)

105. Squadron maintenance crews remove 600gal ferry tanks from one of the 47th's A-10s. (T/Sgt. Plummer, USAF)
106. A live AGM-65B Maverick missile is mounted on to its wing rail beneath an A-10. (T/Sgt. Plummer, USAF)
107. Carrying a practice Maverick – which can be recognized by the absence of guidance fins – a 47th TFS A-10 lands after a training mission. (T/Sgt. Plummer, USAF)

▲108

▲109 ▼110

108. RF-4Cs of the 117th TRW deployed from Birmingham, Alabama, to RAF Coltishall for their summer operations with 'Checkered Flag'. (T/Sgt. Plummer, USAF)

109. A green-coded oxygen bottle is checked as one of the 117th's RF-4s is prepared for a reconnaissance flight. (T/Sgt. Plummer, USAF)

110. An RF-4C of the 123rd TRW, Kentucky ANG, deployed to Ingolstat AB, Germany, for 'Checkered Flag'. Note the wraparound camouflage scheme and the special 'Checkered Flag' rudder markings. (T/Sgt. Plummer, USAF)

111. One of the 123rd's RF-4s tucks its gear away upon leaving the Ingolstat runway. (T/Sgt. Plummer, USAF)

112. An A-7D of the 121st TFW, Ohio ANG, is prepared for a mission during Exercise 'Kindle Liberty', a Central American deployment and training for over-jungle combat in Panama. (S/Sgt. Bandy T. Riley Jr., USAF)

▲113

▲114 ▼115

56

113. Pilots of the 388th TFW taxi their F-16As for take-off during 'Kindle Liberty'. (S/Sgt. Bandy T. Riley Jr., USAF)

114. A Puerto Rican ANG C-7A is refuelled on a Panamanian airstrip. (S/Sgt. Bandy T. Riley Jr., USAF)

115. An EC-130E of the 193rd Electronic Combat Group, from Harrisburg, Pennsylvania, photographed during 'Kindle Liberty'. (S/Sgt. Bandy T. Riley Jr., USAF)

116. AC-130As of the 711th SOS, AFRES, in Panama. (S/Sgt. Bandy T. Riley Jr., USAF)

117. A patrol boat is backed up to a C-5A after completion of the exercises. (S/Sgt. Bandy T. Riley Jr., USAF)

▲118

118. A UH-1P attached to the 56th TFW lands with 'wounded' during 'Patriot Samaritan' medical training exercises at McDill AFB, Florida, in autumn 1983. (S/Sgt. Phil Schmitten, USAF)
119. A 'patient' is moved from a UH-1P helicopter to field medical facilities. (S/Sgt. Phil Schmitten, USAF)
120. USAF F-15s of the 18th TFW fly dissimilar air combat training with F-4EJs of Japan's 310th and 305th Fighter Squadrons during 'Cope North '83–4', one of a series of joint training missions flown from Komatsu AB, Japan. (S/Sgt. Steve McGill, USAF)

▼119　　　　　　　　　　　　　　　　　　　　　　　　　　　　　　　120▶

▲121 ▼122

121. 'Reforger' is an annual deployment of US forces to Europe for NATO's 'Autumn Forge' exercises. Medical equipment and vehicles are here unloaded from a C-130 at Hanau Army Air Field in early September 1983. (S/Sgt. Michael Haggerty, USAF)
122. 7th Cavalry soldiers are transferred by bus from their C-130 at Monchengladbach, Germany. (SM/Sgt. Don Sutherland, USAF)

123. A-10s of the 81st TFW deployed from the UK to Wiesbaden AB, Germany, for the first time in two years during the 'Cold Fire '83' portion of 'Autumn Forge'. (SM/Sgt. Don Sutherland, USAF)
124. A faulty stall warning unit is checked prior to one of the 81st's training missions. (SM/Sgt. Don Sutherland, USAF)

123▼

124▼

▲125

125. A deployment of BGM-109G ground-launched cruise missiles to Britain strengthened NATO's nuclear war capabilities but met with resistance from several civilian factions. (USAF)

126. The US invasion of Grenada in October 1983 will be the subject of debates on international law for years to come. In Operation 'Urgent Fury' Army Rangers and paratroopers, US Marines and USAF Security Police were supported by helicopters and AC-130 gunships as they cleared that island of Cuban troops and engineers following the collapse of Grenada's government and the murder of its Marxist president. The combat was unique in Air Force history since all of its ground strikes were flown by MAC aircraft! TAC F-15s and A-10s were available but not used when it was determined that MAC AC-130s and Army helicopters could secure the combat area. In this photo, members of the 82nd Airborne Division chat following operations, as a 317th MAW C-130 takes off from a Port Salinas runway. (USAF)

127. A 317th MAW C-130 leaves Port Salinas. Soviet-designed transports have been pushed to the grass at the main terminal. (USAF)

128. A 317th MAW C-130 and a grey 1st SOW AC-130 join other air traffic in Barbados during 'Urgent Fury'. (USAF)

129. Mission completed, combat troops board a C-141 to leave Grenada. (USAF)

▼**128**

▼**129**